WITH
HITLER
IN THE WEST

WITH
HITLER
IN THE WEST

HEINRICH HOFFMANN

FOREWORD BY
GENERALFELDMARSCHALL
WILHELM KEITEL
SUPREME HIGH COMMAND OF THE WEHRMACHT

TRANSLATED FROM THE
ORIGINAL THIRD REICH BOOK
'MIT HITLER IM WESTEN'

Pen & Sword
MILITARY

This edition published in 2015 by

Pen & Sword Military
An imprint of
Pen & Sword Books Ltd.
47 Church Street
Barnsley
South Yorkshire
S70 2AS

This book was first published as 'Mit Hitler im Westen'
by Zeitgeschichte-Verlag in Berlin, 1940.

ISBN: 9781473833524

A CIP catalogue record for this book is available from the British Library.

Printed and bound in Malta
By Gutenberg Press Ltd

Pen & Sword Books Ltd. incorporates the imprints of Pen & Sword Aviation, Pen & Sword Family History, Pen
& Sword Maritime, Pen & Sword Military, Pen & Sword Discovery, Pen & Sword Politics, Pen & Sword Atlas,
Pen & Sword Archaeology, Wharncliffe Local History, Wharncliffe True Crime, Wharncliffe Transport, Pen &
Sword Select, Pen & Sword Military Classics, Leo Cooper, The Praetorian Press, Claymore Press, Remember
When, Seaforth Publishing and Frontline Publishing

For a complete list of Pen & Sword titles please contact
PEN & SWORD BOOKS LIMITED
47 Church Street, Barnsley, South Yorkshire, S70 2AS, England
E-mail: enquiries@pen-and-sword.co.uk
Website: www.pen-and-sword.co.uk

FOREWORD

AS DAWN BROKE ON 10TH MAY 1940, the western front was poised for the attack, the German folk and the world awaited the result of the battle with intense expectation and tension. With rock hard confidence in the supreme command,and in their own ability, the army and air force were determined to strike and crush the enemy.

Still fresh in the memory were the lightning landings by the army and air force in Norway, still in the memory too was the daring exploits of the navy in the face of the numerically far larger British fleet.

Would this be a repeat of the rapid triumphant advance through Poland which lasted just eighteen days? Would it be possible, under far more difficult conditions, to strike just as quickly and decisively attack the French and English? Those were the questions to which the world awaited answers in those May days!

As in Poland, the *Führer* and Supreme Command was in once more the midst of his armed forces. From his command post, he directed and observed the actions of the army and of the air force with calm self-assurance. The swift progress of the operations accomplished the projected targets of the campaign and all objectives were achieved on schedule. As the campaign unfolded battles of annihilation unfolded on a hitherto unheralded scale. Holland and Belgium were overrun in a few days. The Maginot Line, considered to be impenetrable, was broken through, whole armies were encircled, destroyed or captured. The British Expeditionary Force was swept from the mainland; it could only save the wreckage of its best divisions by a terrified retreat across the channel. The entrance of the ally Italy into the war now overcame the last resistance of strength of a France already beaten to the ground. France soon saw herself forced to appeal for an armistice. On the summer solstice 1940 the *Führer* in the forest of Compiègne expunged the shame of the armistice of 9th November 1910.

From the North Sea to the Biscay, the Atlantic coast of France the German armed forces now stand at disposal for the decisive struggle against England; the final opponent. Army, navy and air force form the close knit armed brotherhood ready to strive for the accomplishment of the final victory.

With the deepest gratitude we will always remember the man who is the head and heart of this titanic episode and whose brilliant leadership will also bring victory over England. I had the good fortune, during this incomparable triumphant advance of our armed forces in Holland, Belgium and France to stand at the *Führer's* side, to accompany him on front visits and to discover with him, not just the battlefield upon which his soldiers had triumphed in this war, but also those upon which German warriors fought and died in the World War 1914-1918.

This pictorial work 'With Hitler in the West' was conceived to preserve a record of this unique triumphant battle. This should give the German folk the highlights of the military event which began from the point where the *Führer* made his decisions, and encompassed the time the *Führer* spent time with his victorious troops. I trust that the German folk and above all the German youth will recognise a true testament to the accomplishment of leadership and fighting men!

GENERALFELDMARSCHALLL &
SUPREME HIGH COMMAND OF THE WEHRMACHT

One the morning of 10th May 1940. Assault infantry gather before the attack.

Across the border. Tank obstacles do not stop the grenadiers of a Panzer Division.

The enemy was a master of destruction. But that does not stop the German advance.

Jump up, advance - advance!

Look out, tanks! The time for our tank-hunters has arrived.

The artillery has done its duty. The infantry finishes the task. An assault troop is about to infiltrate.

Assault troops move up to the front.

Advance under burning heat. German fliers and German artillery have done a thorough job here.

Assault troops in a battle damaged town.

Infantry assembled in a captured town.

Prisoners file out of the fortified works formerly defended by them.

Here the spoils of war are used as cover.

Houses set ablaze by the enemy do not hinder the advance of our troops.

By both day and night marches our infantry, pursue the enemy.

The crews bring their guns forward.

The ubiquitous infantry! Queen of the battlefield!

Paratroopers land in Holland, 10th May 1940.

The jump!

Paratroopers and infantrymen of the airborne troops assemble for the attack on Rotterdam.

Paratroopers attack!

The Knights Cross direct from the hand of the *Führer*.

The *Führer* and the heroes of Eban Emael.

The enemy refuses surrender. Forcing an attack against Rotterdam.

Burning harbour facilities in the city of Rouen on the Seine.

So here we see how German fliers hit the target!

A thoroughly destroyed rail bridge over the Albert canal.

This is England's fault. The oil tanks of Rotterdam burn.

Fliers and Panzer crews meet up with each other.

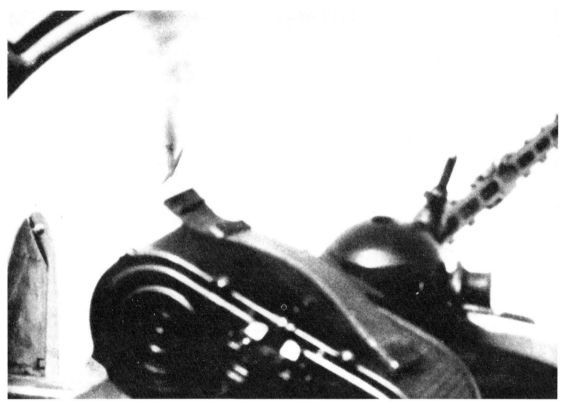

End of a French fighter.

Attack the enemy!

German warplanes over Paris, left the Arc de Triomphe.

A View of Beauvois in ruins.

Artillery that was destroyed by Stukas.

Much of France's air force was already destroyed on the ground.

The face of the German pilot.

Burning ships in the harbour of Rotterdam.

This is how the *Felsennest* (Rocky Eyrie headquarters) of the *Führer* was camouflaged.

Generalfeldmarschall Karl Rudolf Gerd von Rundstedt delivers a report to the *Führer*.

The *Führer* with *Reichsmarschall* Göring.
The *Führer's* chief military adjutant, Colonel Schmundt, at a presentation.

The *Reichsmarschall* has appeared at headquarters to make a report.

Reichsmarschall Göring with the *Führer* at the 'Rocky Eyrie' headquarters.

The Supreme Commander leaves the map room.

At the morning presentation in the 'Rocky Eyrie' headquarters. *Generalfeldmarschall* Keitel and Chief of the Armed Forces Leadership Office, General of the Artillery Jodl.

The *Führer's* living quarters in the 'Rocky Eyrie'.

The *Führer* and his Reich Press Chief, Dr. Dietrich.

The *Führer* in a conference with his chief military adjutant, Colonel D. G. Schmundt.

The camouflaged 'Rocky Eyrie'.

Masterfully concealed from sight on ground and from the air.

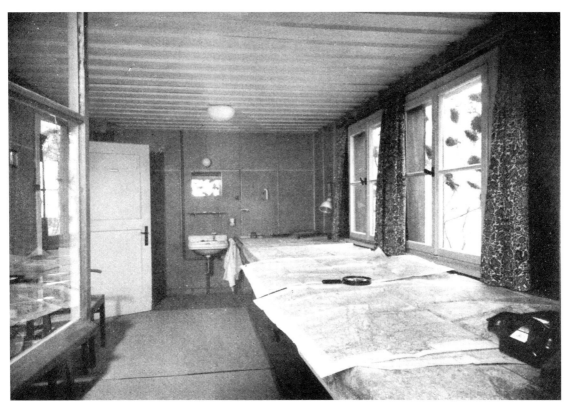

The map room in the 'Rocky Eyrie'.

The *Führer's* constant support staff in the headquarters.

A visit to the front: Cheering soldiers great their Supreme Commander.

On a visit to the front.

Receipt of a report during a front visit.

This is what Lille looked like after the capture by German troops.

Evidence of the street fighting in Lille.

Battlefield of the Great War on the Vimy Ridge.

The *Führer* fought in this area in the Great War.

The Commanding General of an Army Corps, General of the Artillery Heitz, explains to the *Führer* the course of the fighting of the last days, also present is the Army Commander, *Generalfeldmarschall* von Kluge.

The *Führer* visits the Canadian monument on the Vimy Ridge...

... and the Loretto Height.
A celebrated Army Commander, General Field-Marshal von Kluge, accompanies the *Führer*.

At the field kitchen.

Senior General von Küchler, Supreme Commander of an Army, at a presentation.

On the Vimy Ridge.

At a visit to old positions of the Great War. Short look at the Allied monument in Ypres.

The *Führer* visits the graves of German soldiers in Flanders. On the right of the *Führer* is the Commanding General of an Army Corps, General of the Infantry von Schwedler.

Silent remembrance at the cemetery for the heroes of Langemarck.

Inspecting the old French fortification works.

'Totally destroyed...'

Destroyed heavy French tanks tasked with defending a village.

German crews after the victorious battle.

A short rest after the battle.

That common end of many English tanks.

The German Panzer commandant.

Escaped from hell.

Senior General Guderian, leader of a Panzer group, on a reconnaissance trip.

Heavy anti-aircraft guns in ground combat with French tanks.

'Panzer-March'. The first wave of the attack rolls forward.

The *Führer* meets *Generalfeldmarschall* Kesselring. In the background, *Generalfeldmarschall* von Brauchitsch and *Generalfeldmarschall* von Bock.

The *Führer* in conversation with *Generalfeldmarschall* von Kluge and Major-General Rommel, the Commander of a Panzer division.

In conversation with Senior General Strauss.

At the airport Brussels-Evere. *Generalfeldmarschall* von Bock reports to the *Führer*, accompanied by *Generalfeldmarschall* von Brauchitsch.

The *Führer* in conversation with his soldiers.

They greet him on the path of victory.

Meeting a Special Officer of a propaganda company. Behind them, *Generalfeldmarschall* von Reichenau and Lieutenant-General Bodenschatz.

At the train station of a border crossing.

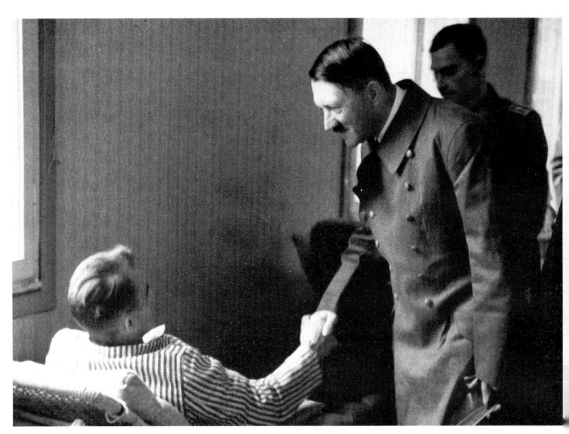

His concern for the wounded.

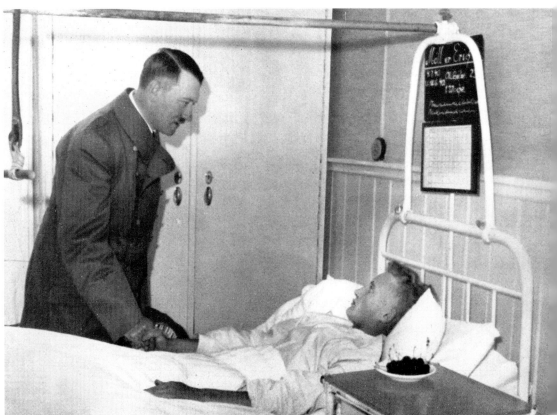

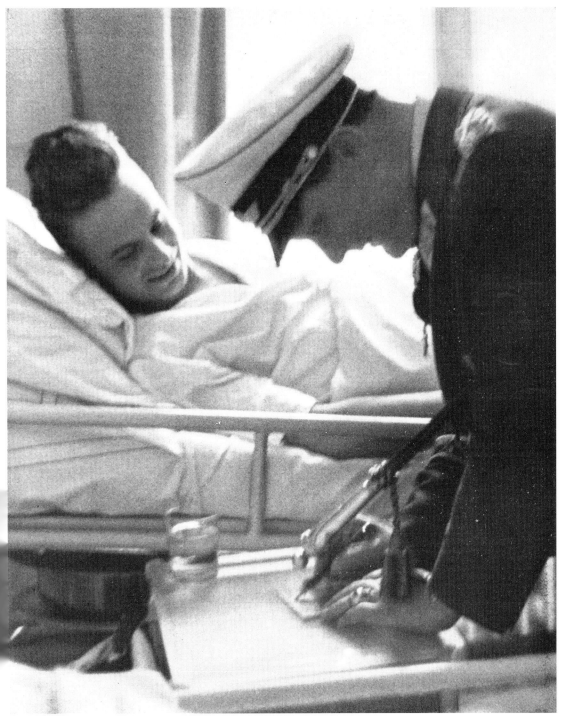

Reichsmarschall Göring too cheers up the wounded with his visit.

The work of the gunners is strenuous. Every man must do his bit.

Heavy artillery moves into position.

A German mortar in firing position.

This is German rail artillery.

A rail gun firing.

A triumph of German weapons technology.

This is the language of modern warfare.

The most modern listening equipment...

and a spotlights detachment...

... support our anti-aircraft artillery.

It was from here, in the Ardennes, the *Führer* directed the operations.

The second *Führer* headquarters 'Wolf's Lair'.

Reichsmarschall Göring leaves the 'Wolf's Lair' headquarters after reporting to the *Führer*.

At headquarters, the *Führer* briefs his old comrade Minister Rudolf Hess on the situation.

Reichsmarschall Göring takes his leave from the *Führer* in order to return in the 'Stork' to his headquarters.

In the 'Wolf's Lair'. The Supreme Commander of the Army reports new successes to the *Führer*.

Generalfeldmarschall von Brauchitsch at a conference. From left to right: Major Deyhle, General of the Artillery Jodl, the Supreme Commander of the Army von Brauchitsch, Grand Admiral Dr. H. C. Raeder. Far left: *Generalfeldmarschall* Keitel.

In the 'Wolf's Lair', Emissary Hewel of the Foreign Office gives the *Führer* a report.

On the path to the map room. Grand Admiral Dr. H. C. Raeder and *Generalfeldmarschall* Brauchitsch have come for a conference.

The *Führer* in the 'Wolf's Lair'.

New reports have come. The *Führer* plots them on the map himself.

After the morning situation report in the 'Wolf's Lair'.
In the background the house of the Armed Forces Leadership Staff.

They sail against England.

A German U-boat approaches a French harbour.

A typical German U-boat sailor after a long trip.

An English troop transport goes to the bottom of the sea.

The English aircraft carrier Courageous, fell victim to a German torpedo.

The crew of an English destroyer is rescued by Germans under most trying conditions.

Battle on high sea.

English destroyers set ablaze.

A minesweeper passes the wreck of a lost English ship.

Speedboats on a combat mission.

The beach at Dunkirk after the flight of the English.

The 'victorious' retreat of the English.

This is not how they imagined the march to Berlin.

There are captured helmets beyond counting. Here is a French specimen collection.

French armoured scout vehicles that were abandoned in panic in the march column.

Enemy warships destroyed by Stukas in the harbour of Dunkirk.

A scene on the beach of Dunkirk. That was once English anti-aircraft artillery.

German destroyers fly over Dunkirk which is under fire.

The downhearted survivors of the war mongers.

That is war.

Misery for the refugees.

The retreat routes of the English-French Army.

A captured French Army Commander is taken to Germany by plane.

The visit of the German negotiator to the Belgian headquarters.

The Belgian Army capitulates. Arrival of a negotiator.

The Belgian Army capitulates. A German negotiator in the Belgian headquarters.

Destruction wrought by the enemy during his retreat...

but Major-General Dr. Todt with his staff...

... and his men are soon repairing the destroyed roads.

The Organisation Todt building bridges and roads.

Shell craters are cleared up.

These are the men of the Organisation Todt.

Shortly before the truce goes in to effect. The *Führer* and his entourage hear the announcement of the pending truce as it is broadcast over the radio.

'Germany, Germany above all!'

'We assemble to pray'. Proclamation of the truce in the *Führer's* headquarters on June 25th, 1940, 01:35.

Entry of German troops into Paris on June 15th, 1940. German artillery on the Place de la Concorde.

A Regimental Commander receives the march past.

Men from Lower Saxony at the Arc de Triomphe.

Advancing, past endless columns of prisoners.

English and French prisoners in the harbour of Dunkirk.

Refugee misery in Flanders. The relief column from Bayern mollifies the greatest distress.

The action of our transport airplanes for the wounded.

In his quarters from 1916.

The *Führer* inspects his old quarters from 1916, with two comrades, Reich Leader Amann and Ernst Schmied.

In the church of Laon.

Anti-tank soldiers protect the infantry crossings.

Military engineers, prepare for the river crossing.

Crossing on inflated rafts.

This is how the heavy bunkers of the Maginot Line were smoked out.
The assault troop waits for the garrison to surrender.

The *Führer* in the Upper Front front sector.
Inspection of a German bunker unsuccessfully bombarded by the French.

Despite the heaviest artillery fire, the German bunker stands safe and sound.

On the Rhine bridge at Kehl. The *Führer* steps in to German Strassburg.
On the right of the Fuhrer is the Supreme Commander of an Army, Senior General Dollmann.

A French Rhine bunker after bombardment.
Behind the *Führer* are *Generalfeldmarschall* Keitel and Reich Leader Bormann.

In the Vosges at the gorge pass. The Supreme Commander of an Army, Senior General Dollman, explains the course of the heavy fighting to the *Führer*.

In the Vosges. A captured French war horse encounters the *Führer*.

In the Strassburg cathedral.

Paris. On the Trocadero. In the background the Eiffel Tower.

Napoleon's tomb at Les Invalides.

The *Führer* leaves St. Madelaine.
On the left of the *Führer* are Prof. Speer and Prof. Giesler, on the right of the *Führer* is Prof. Breker.

A stroll through the Paris opera house.

The immense booty of the great battle.

French oil tanks are taken into German service.

In the captured equipment dumps.

The quantity of enemy war equipment is enormous.

Inspection of the proceeds. Stacking the artillery munitions.

One of the destroyed French 72-ton tanks.

Captured French rail guns.

Motorised French heavy artillery.

After the peace offer of the French.

Discussion between both leaders of the Axis Powers in Munich.

Compiègne, 1940.

The *Führer* at the memorial stone that was designed to immortalise the humiliation of 1918.

The French delegation poses in front of the historic railcar for the beginning of the negotiations.

On 21st June, the *Führer* receives the French delegation.

Generalfeldmarschall Keitel reads aloud the *Führer's* preamble.

To the sound of the German National Anthem, the *Führer* leaves the site of the negotiations.

The first troops returning home at the Brandenburg Gate after the victory over France.

This is how Greater Germany welcomes its victorious troops home. A Brandenburg division returns to the Homeland after the victorious campaign in France.

The *Führer* passes through the lavishly decorated streets of the capital city to the Reich Chancellery.

The *Führer* and *Reichsmarschall* Göring on the historic balcony of the Reich Chancellery.

The grateful people. Jubilation surrounds the *Führer* in front of the Reich Chancellery on 6th July, 1940.

The historic Reichstag session on 19th July, 1940.

The *Führer's* thanks to his *Reichsmarschall*.